The Art of Imperfection

By Véronique Vienne with photographs by Erica Lennard

The Art of Imperfection

SIMPLE WAYS TO MAKE PEACE WITH YOURSELF

Clarkson Potter/Publishers
New York

Published by Clarkson Potter/Publishers, 201 East 50th Street, New York, New York 10022.
Member of the Crown Publishing Group.

Random House, Inc. New York, Toronto, London, Sydney, Auckland
www.randomhouse.com

CLARKSON N. POTTER, POTTER, and colophon are registered trademarks of Random House, Inc.

Printed in Japan

Design by Maggie Hinders based on a design by Skouras Design.

Library of Congress Cataloging-in-Publication Data

Vienne, Véronique.
The art of imperfection: simple ways to make peace with yourself / by Véronique Vienne;
with photographs by Erica Lennard—1st ed.
Includes bibliographical references.
1. Conduct of life. 2. Imperfection I. Title.
BJ1595.V54 1999
158.1—dc21 99-24938

ISBN 0-609-60521-6

10 9 8 7 6 5 4

DEDICATION

To the spirit of *La Bohème*

ACKNOWLEDGMENTS

We would like to thank the people who prompted us to do something beyond *The Art of Doing Nothing:* our agent, Helen Forson Pratt; our editor, Annetta Hanna; and our creative director, Marysarah Quinn: We also would like to credit the women and men who helped make our imperfect project such a perfect endeavor: Brooks Adams and Lisa Liebman; Alexandra; Roberto Bergero; Jane Burd; Silvy Fleury; Laurie Frank; Charlie Griffin; Maggie Hinders; Patricia Tartour Jonathan; Elizabeth, Mathilda, and Emily Kime; Scarlett and Michele Lamy; Mak; Outa Mascolo and Michele Laverdac; Audrey Matson; Maya; Sophie Pierlot; Lise Ryall; Claudia Van Rysen; and Virginia Witbeck—with homage to Simone de Beauvoir, Marguerite Duras, Diana Vreeland, and Coco Chanel. And *un très grand merci* to our husbands, Denis Colomb and Bill Young, for their support and vision.

CONTENTS

We are loved for who we are, imperfections and all.

Our innate idiosyncrasies are actually more endearing to others than our most glorious personal achievements.

You're a great cook, but your sweetheart falls in love with you the day you set the stove on fire with your crème brûlée. You're a smart lawyer, but your kids adore you because you make scary faces. You've just been elected president of the board, but your best friend says, "You fooled them, didn't you?"

Make peace with yourself once and for all: Love is not a meritocracy.

History is full of incompetent people who were beloved, blunderers with winsome personality traits, and inept folks who delighted their entourages with their unassuming presences. Their secret? To accept their flaws with the same grace and humility as their best qualities.

There are practical benefits to not being perfect. As scientists today are discovering, quirkiness is a creative force in nature, one capable of neutralizing the otherwise irreversible process of degradation called entropy. In the same way, our faults, weaknesses, and unlucky breaks work to our advantage by making us more resilient, more inventive, and ultimately more efficient.

Think of this book as a series of friendly exhortations that will help you find solace in your shortcomings and even celebrate your most embarrassing lapses. No, you don't have to be perfect to be a successful human being. In fact, more often than not, the desire to be right interferes with things getting better, and the need to be in control increases disorder and chaos.

Forgive yourself. Soon, you will discover that self-acceptance and tolerance do not have to be hard work.

1

the art of making mistakes

Imagine a different world, one in which people do not spend an inordinate amount of energy fuming against their fate each time they make a mistake. A world in which one takes for granted that if things can go wrong, they probably will.

It would be so civilized. Folks would bump into furniture, miss deadlines, get lost on the way to the airport, forget to return phone calls, and show up at

Chaos follows precise rules and patterns.

parties a day early, without getting unduly annoyed with themselves.

You and I would not be personally insulted when we dropped the sugar bowl on the floor, backed the car into the mailbox, burned the dinner while on the phone, or failed to meet our quarterly projections.

Dream on. This forgiving world is as utopian a vision as Shangri-La. Though we all agree that to err is human, each of us individually believes that he or she is the exception. What's good enough for you isn't good enough for me. Make a mistake? Not on my watch!

We are convinced that getting it right is a matter of survival. Surrounded as we are by machines, we feel that we must perform flawlessly to stay ahead of the game. An industrial-age mentality keeps us all on the steep and narrow path of productivity.

Unfortunately, thinking that being right will save us from being wrong is a misapprehension. While, in the last decade, we have labored to be as accurate as our machines, these same machines have been redesigned to be as impulsive as we are. Today, some of the most advanced electronic devices, from satellites to pacemakers, are engineered to be partly inconsistent, in accordance with the dramatic findings of "chaos scientists."

These complexity experts, as they are also called, believe that small errors can counteract the curse of the second law of thermodynamics—a well-established physics principle that dictates that everything in the universe must eventually cool down and decay.

Today, in various fields, from space exploration to stock market predictions, computers are programmed to be quirky on purpose, in an attempt to undo the slumping effects of universal entropy. A case in point is an energy-efficient Japanese dishwasher, designed to be "chaotic," that gets china, glass, and silverware cleaner by using two rotating arms that spin erratically.

In our day and age, the irrational is on the cutting edge. More and more, you are likely to run into people who will explain to you that you are wrong—that everything you've known so far is up for grabs. Whether they are linguists or cosmologists, computer hackers or neuroscientists, investment brokers or mathematicians, they all seem to believe that progress is knowing less and less about more and more.

And so you listen to them. By the end of the conversation, you too will be convinced that better is the enemy of good. And that it takes a long time to understand nothing.

What a bummer? Not at all. Letting go of basic assumptions is as exciting as looking at the earth from space. You feel something like a delicious vertigo, a sense of weightlessness. For a short but blissful moment you experience a reprieve from the gravitational pull of your nineteenth-century ego.

Next time you break a plate, or lose your keys, or jump to false conclusions, why not take it in stride? Consider the possibility that there is a hidden pattern behind your random acts of blunderism.

DON'T BE A WISE GUY

Paradoxically, the best time to learn from your mistakes is before they happen. When you set an appointment, knowing you are going to cancel it at the last minute. When you agree to do a job you are not qualified to do. When you take a second helping, though you promised yourself you wouldn't.

Admit it: At that moment you know you are making the wrong move.

Ignoring your gut feelings, you go ahead.

Ask for forgiveness, not permission.

decide, against your best judgment, to do the wrong thing. One can never second-guess this mysterious urge to override all the evidence.

Like the erratic movements of the rotating arm of the dishwasher, miscalculations can make the machine more efficient. The same could be said of the unpredictable swirl of leaves in autumn, the random elegance of clouds, or the imperfect symmetry of a beautiful face. Never underestimate what looks like a fumble.

Take a moment to wonder at the uniqueness of the mistakes you are about to make.

Feel the thrill as you buy that over-the-top, low-cut red dress.

Be outrageous—and slam that door.

As you do so, remind yourself that your recklessness is nothing but the expression of a cosmic urge to challenge the general tendency of things to ebb toward a lukewarm and boring equilibrium.

Even if you fall flat on your face, you figure, you'll pull yourself back together. It is your prerogative, as a human being, to be able to

What's Wrong with This Picture?

In art and architecture, what looks like a mistake is often a deliberate signal meant to attract the attention of insiders to a particular aspect of the work.

- In Islamic art, small flaws abound in what look like the most luxurious carpets, pottery, and mosaics. Artists are urged to make mistakes on purpose, to remind observers that God alone is perfection.

- In the Zen tradition, "wabi-sabi" objects, carefully crafted to be intentionally imperfect, impermanent, or incomplete, are considered most beautiful—their humble elegance transcending fads and fashion.

- In music, notes that deviate from an established pattern are often used to create emotional tension. Beethoven was fond of this technique. In the Third Symphony's "Funeral March," for example, he replaced sounds with silences to express the mounting sense of sorrow in the piece.

- In literature, James Joyce was the champion of the intentional error. For him, mistakes were "portals of discovery." In *Ulysses* in particular, typos, misspellings, and absence of punctuation add to the insightfulness of his prose.

Even stones are in a state of becoming.

the art of being shy

I t's a good thing we don't know how attractive we are. We would run the risk of becoming arrogant and losing the most endearing of all qualities—lack of self-importance.

When pressed, we will confess to having a few agreeable anatomical features, such as nice shoulders, strong legs, or slender ankles, but most of us grossly underestimate our physical appeal. We are never fully

aware of our real charms—the way we sip our tea, the way we sing off-key, the way we dance till three.

Let's be frank: We all are shy. In private, most of us have unflattering opinions of our physiques. With reason. We are constantly reminded that our bodies don't measure up to stringent contemporary standards of perfection. So much so that on bad days our inner mirrors would have us believe that we are pigeon-breasted and hunchbacked—like the gargoyles of Notre Dame.

No matter how hard we try, compensating for our alleged narcissism by either under-rating or overrating our appearance, we never get it right. Comparing ourselves with media images that bear very little resemblance to the way we look, we become frustrated with bodies that leave a lot to be desired.

For once, though, the media is not to blame for our dim view of ourselves. In this instance, nature is the culprit: We are de-signed to be partially sighted creatures. Take a look at yourself: Your eyes are facing forward, like headlights. You can't turn your gaze inward. If you lean over your chest, you can stare at your navel—but that's as far up as you can go. Over and above it, your nose gets in the way.

Limited vision ensures that we keep our attention on what's out there, in front of us, and makes us less likely to chase our tails. Unless fitted with rear- and side-view mirrors, we can't see our bodies—they are hidden in our blind spots.

Animals depend on their eyes, but also on their senses of smell, taste, or sound, to map out the world. But for human beings, seeing is believing. We insist on making visual contact. If a thing is concealed, it automatically arouses our interest. The parts of our body we can't see are objects of intense curiosity.

To satisfy our inquisitiveness, we had to

wait for the end of the seventeenth century, when full-length mirrors were at long last perfected.

The result of a technological breakthrough in glassmaking, the silver-coated marvels heralded a period of intense visual exploration. The telescope and the microscope were invented at about the same time.

While scientists were investigating unseen worlds, "visibilizing" the invisible universe, ordinary people were able, for the first time in recorded history, to see that other hidden realm—their very own shapes and forms, in their entirety, from head to toe.

Today, catching a glimpse of one's reflected image is a common enough occurrence, yet we still hesitate before recognizing the person in the mirror as our alter ego. Fixing our likeness in the eyes, we see someone who looks as surprised as we do.

And on the rare occasion when we get a chance to peer into a three-way mirror, the

I see my reflection, therefore I am.

sight is even more startling. Just a few feet away stands a perfect stranger—an identical twin we didn't know existed.

"It is as hard to see one's self as to look backward without turning around."
—Henry David Thoreau

The invention of photography only added another layer of confusion to this identity crisis. Unlike painted portraits, which gave sitters plenty of time to settle down into their official personae, snapshots capture awkward instants of self-consciousness. Most of us pore over pictures of ourselves with the same aching trepidation we feel when looking at old photographs of long-lost friends.

Short of hiring a film crew to make a home movie, you and I will never meet our visible selves, the cloned impersonators who act on our behalf.

In the meantime, let's not pretend that we are secure in our self-image. While we are at it, let's ignore the latest theories on self-acceptance and self-esteem that want us to celebrate the way we look. None of us really knows what we look like, so why get all worked up about it?

We might as well accept our fate: We are stuck forever in a zone of invisibility. But come to think of it, it is the safest place to be. By staying right there, away from our own scrutiny, we will never feel less attractive than we are in reality.

THINK WITH THE WHOLE BODY

Paradoxically, the body part we trust the most is one we have never seen: our gray matter. Hidden from sight, exiled under a protective shell, deprived of pain receptors so it never hurts, the brain is considered our most dependable ally.

Our mistake. A bundle of neural cells, the brain has a distorted view of the body it is supposed to control. According to the internal map laid out in the somatosensory cortex, our lips, tongues, noses, fingers, and eyes are huge. Our thumbs are next to our eyes. Our foreheads are tiny, while our jaws are spectacular. Our legs and trunks are elongated. And big fig leaves would not be large enough to cover our private parts.

Yet most of us are convinced that this very cortex is the headquarters of our reason. We owe this wild notion to René Descartes, author of the famous phrase *cogito, ergo sum*—"I think, therefore I am." A French curmudgeon who lived alone, cared for no one, slept till noon, and spent most of his day ruminating in bed, he professed complete disregard for the body, which he described as a mere vehicle for the spirit.

His success was our undoing. To this day, many of us suffer from frequent Cartesian attacks, mild psychotic episodes during which we take for granted that there is a dualistic split between mind and matter, reason and flesh, thoughts and feelings.

Like Descartes, we assume that the body is nothing more than a convenience carrier for the brain. From the neck down, we are a means to an end. The main function of our physical being is to haul the mind from appointment to appointment, while feeding it a lot of sugar and carbohydrates to keep it on a continuous high.

If that's the case—if indeed the body is but a glorified grocery cart—then it doesn't need to be so large, so complicated, or so finely tuned. Why would nature support such a superfluous flesh-and-bones contraption when a simple container with a couple of wheels would do?

Our present fascination with thinness could be an indication that nature is testing the idea of downsizing our physical operating system. With the help of cyberspace, the mind is gaining more and more power—and so, the evolutionary trend toward body shrinkage makes more and more sense.

Some of us gallantly fight back by grow-

The dualistic split between mind and matter is an optical illusion.

ing corpulent, robust, and stalwart. But unless all of us, as a culture, find a way to reconcile body and mind, sooner or later even the most majestic among us will have to give up their voluptuous curves and get on with the curtailment program.

Whether you think that you are too thin or too fat, don't bother going on a diet. Counting calories doesn't work. Instead, come down from your mental perch and get reacquainted with your physical self.

Exercise helps—and so does closing your eyes and visualizing the Oneness of It All. But for expediency, try the following: Stand up straight, take a deep breath, and give René Descartes the finger.

The Etiquette of Shyness

You can be excruciatingly self-conscious and still cut a dashing figure. Just follow the rules of etiquette that were established for that purpose, and you will be able to negotiate the first minute of an introduction as gracefully as if you were the most experienced man-about-town.

- Look ahead when entering a room.
- Take a second to draw your weight up, loosen your arms, and open your chest.
- Make eye contact with people by focusing on either their right or their left eyes (at short range, it's impossible to focus on both eyes at the same time).
- Smile at people—it will unclench your teeth and relax your face.
- Be the first to say hello.
- As soon as you introduce yourself, initiate a handshake by deliberately extending your hand.
- Firmly take hold of the other person's hand and shake *three* times.
- Just as deliberately, open your hand and bring it back down to your side.

Dare to overdress: Be poised with panache.

the art of looking like yourself

The best beauty product is to have a life. A real life. With challenges, disappointments, stress, and laughter. The much-touted inner beauty is a natural radiance that comes as a result of mental and emotional involvement. The increased demand for oxygen of a busy brain attracts blood to the head, resulting in a luminous bloom on your forehead and cheeks. Your complexion glows, your eyes shine,

and your lips look more voluptuous. Probably the most effective beauty regimen is to get up in the morning and say "Wow."

Coco Chanel, who unwittingly became the symbol of one of the most prestigious beauty companies in the world, used to say, "When I am bored, I am a thousand years old." She believed that nature gives you the face you have at twenty, but that you give yourself the face you have at fifty. If you had no wrinkles, no crow's-feet, and no smile lines, chances are you'd let life pass you by. "Women should have pleasurable flaws," she'd quip.

One of women's most pleasurable flaws has to be their excessive imagination. When asked, in skin-care tests, to try a so-called new miracle cream, the majority of female users are enthusiastic about the results. Even when they are unknowingly testing a placebo cream containing no special ingredient, 50 percent say that they look much better—baf-fling researchers who see no real changes to their skin's texture.

Beauty is in the eye of the beholder, and in the eye of the woman who holds the mirror. This is nothing new—Shakespeare alluded to this capricious "judgment of the eye." But repeated clinical evidence of the phenomenon, as observed in countless double-blind, placebo-controlled scientific experiments, is forcing us to redefine what we call beauty.

Walk through the cosmetics department at your local store, and marvel at the eagerness of customers to embrace the outlandish claims of an age-defying night cream, the moisturizing benefits of a lipstick, or the firming properties of a foundation.

When buying beauty products that support the power of their imagination, women are subverting the notion that there are absolute standards of beauty by which they can be judged. Men are wising up, too. By embracing cosmetic lines directed at them, men show that they are eager to avoid being stereotyped as well.

And not a minute too soon. Beauty is not a physical thing anymore. It is no longer the sum total of visible, positive attributes—it can only be characterized by an absence of negative judgment.

A case in point: the postmodern language used by copywriters to describe the elusive benefits of beauty products. A makeup "helps retexturize invisibility." A cream "reduces the visible appearance of imperfections." And, oh, yes—"You'll love what you don't see," claims an antiwrinkle cream.

It's all a disappearing act. But what is removed in this process of elimination are not the blemishes but the blame—the shame and the embarrassment that were associated with traditional aesthetic evaluations.

Invisible beauty lets your real face shine through.

Today, mothers and daughters are about the same age.

Old-fashioned imperfections are no longer seen as flaws. Plastic surgeons report that today a growing number of older women who had their noses done when they were

Beauty is a mystery hidden in the shadow of our youth.

young are going back under the knife, asking for their "real" noses to be rebuilt—no longer ashamed of the larger, bonier organs they used to despise.

Cancer survivors get a new lease on life by flaunting their recovery from what was once a shameful illness. With shorter haircuts, brighter lipsticks, or blonder manes, they celebrate their extraordinary beauty.

And you and I are reappraising our high-school days, with a new fondness for the gawky teenagers we once were. Come to think of it, next time we get a haircut, why not take our yearbooks along, and ask the stylists to imitate the wavy shag or the teased-up bob we used to think was cool.

THE RULES OF
REALHOOD

The ideal of beauty is replaced today by an ideal of realness. Stylists, colorists, hairdressers, and makeup artists have figured out how to help all of us real folks out there reclaim our realhood—and still feel glamorous.

Traditional makeovers are ridiculed. "Makeunders" are introduced as the next thing. Today, cosmetics are used not to hide but, on the contrary, to reveal the slight unevenness and asymmetry of your face.

Your complexion is evened out with barely noticeable dabs of foundation. The trick is to smooth the texture of the skin without totally airbrushing its grain or erasing the small scars, tiny lesions, and fine lines that show that you have a life—and a past.

Although flawless skin is no longer a prerequisite, getting rid of frizzy hair is non-negotiable. With proper exertion, the most recalcitrant mane is subdued into a glossy headpiece. Once straightened, though, locks are mussed up. One of the tenets of this new authentic beauty concept is that you must look like you never bother with mirrors, brushes, and combs.

But the most revealing telltale sign of realhood is an underaccessorized look. Big jewelry is ostracized. Scarves are proscribed. Hats are frowned upon. Handbags are eliminated. Simplicity is key—and stylists urge you to discard anything that might distract from your new real face.

Gone are the days when a little bad taste was like a nice splash of paprika.

Though there is nothing intrinsically wrong with being tastefully made up and quietly attired, you and I had better think twice before adopting standards of perfect imperfection that can become just as oppressive as standards of perfect perfection.

Reality Check

When at long last you meet the love of your life, see Venice, or get what you always wanted, you feel like pinching yourself. No, you are not dreaming. In fact, you are probably having a heightened moment of awareness. The real thing often looks unreal.

To go beyond the illusion of ordinary reality, try the following:

- **Close your eyes:** Though we usually take pictures to make an occasion more special, we can also fix the impression forever in our memories by closing our eyes and savoring the moment with our other senses.

- **Mute your mind:** We all keep a running commentary in our heads, hoping that words will make what we see more real. But it's usually at the end of the day, when we are too tired to think, that reality begins to sink in.

- **Confuse your sense of direction:** Thinking you know where you are often robs you of the experience of reality. To explore a new place without preconceived ideas, take along a compass instead of a map.

- **Miss the action:** Rather than visit all of Paris in three days, just see one museum, and spend the rest of your time sitting in cafés and gardens, dreaming, reading, and watching the crowd.

Life is but a dream.

the art of having nothing to wear

Style is to clothes what carbon dating is to archaeologists and geologists: a sure way to tell when something was created. But while measuring the amount of radiocarbon in an organism reveals how old it is, style in a garment reveals how young it makes you feel.

The more style there is in clothes, the more buoyant the feeling.

In fashion, the ultimate challenge is to strike a balance between two extremes: timelessness and timeliness. More often than not, though, clothes last a lot longer than the youthful spirit in which they were created. Think about it this way: Radiocarbon in fabric has a half-life of 5,730 years—give or take 40 years. The style of an outfit is subjective, elusive, and volatile, with a half-life of less than two months.

This discrepancy makes for a lot of clothes in mint condition languishing on racks in closets, storage spaces, thrift shops, costume rental stores, attics, and museums. It also makes for a lot of us feeling guilty: Our closets are full, yet we can never find the right thing to wear.

Some garments, arguably, keep their appeal for months, even years. Yet one day, unexpectedly, their style expires in your arms as you put them on. Really good clothes can turn matronly within weeks. And quite a few outfits look trite the minute you take them out of their tissue-paper cocoon and snip off their price tags.

In women's wear in particular, the demise of style is sudden and irreversible. If you insist on wearing a garment that has lost its *je ne sais quoi,* you run the risk of feeling as dated as a six-hundred-million-year-old trilobite.

Remember your favorite, above-the-knee, black leather skirt? Inexplicably, it became extinct in October 1991—in what now feels like the late Precambrian. The red sequined top you bought for New Year's Eve 1997 was history by Valentine's Day. A wide-lapel jacket you got on sale at the end of May 1998, at a 40 percent markdown, looked like an archaeological find a month later.

To be sure, clothes are best understood when viewed on a geological time scale. They make most sense as artifacts designed to help us keep track of passing seasons, years,

A walking encyclopedia: Your shoes know everything about you.

and decades. You can measure a lifetime in silhouette adjustments, hemline revolutions, retro-fads—and how often the miniskirt craze came and went. Fashion is most useful as an instrument of measure, a way to monitor intervals between historical events.

The twentieth century will endure through Coco Chanel's little black dress, Simone de Beauvoir's turbans, Jacqueline Kennedy's sunglasses, Marilyn Monroe's

Fashion is the best over-the-counter youth prescription.

"Happy Birthday, Mr. President" sequined sheath, Diane von Furstenberg's wrap chemises, Jane Fonda's striped leotards, Nancy Reagan's red power suits, and Imelda Marcos's shoes.

Look inside your closet: Each item in it is an entry in your sartorial diary—each chronicles a moment in your personal history. As self-defining as the clothes you bought last week are those you no longer care for. They tell where you came from, when you got here, and who you've become. They are part of the long autobiographical narrative that makes your life unique. Diana Vreeland, the legendary editor of *Vogue* magazine in the sixties, once said, "Where would fashion be without literature?"

Don't worry if you wear only a fraction of the clothes you own. Your invisible wardrobe is the underpinning of your present style. Though not on display, the frocks or suits you've discarded have left an indeli-ble imprint on the way you dress today. Without them, you could never have picked the three or four outfits that, you now feel, best capture the essence of who you are.

STYLE IS KNOWING WHAT NOT TO WEAR

The larger your disposable income, the greater your need to know what not to wear. "Elegance is refusal," said the imperious Vreeland. On the list of raiment to leave on the racks are clothes that are a little too tight, jackets with pockets in all the wrong places, garments that ride up instead of down, and trousers you think fit you because you can zip them up.

Men show great savvy in this domain. Masculine tailoring is designed to smooth physical flaws. Women have no such luck:

their garments are not as user-friendly. To look good, they depend on the dos and don'ts of fashion.

For instance, femmes fatales blessed with curves learn the hard way to stay away from double-breasted jackets—overlapping lapels add too much buildup to their chests. Eventually they dare to wear snug garments that are a lot more flattering to their fuller figures than loose tunics and pants.

Try as they might, though, women should not look forward to ever getting it right. In the long run, it wouldn't work to their advantage. A case in point is the Duchess of Windsor, who overcame her many physical flaws to become one of the most elegant women of her time. She never managed to look vulnerable, though. In fact, she was always so perfectly put together that intimate observers began to suspect that her punctiliousness was designed to hide the fact that she was a man!

The lure of perfection is pernicious. It preys on the best of us. And it strikes its victims swiftly. One morning, you absentmindedly put on your trusted white blouse. Your beige suit. Your pearl necklace. Your good Italian loafers. That day, feeling overly confident, you walk past the most delicious peach acetate stretch satin shirt in a store, without even noticing. Your brain registers no sense of possibilities, no secret yearning, no desire for fetching frills.

A year later, it's too late. You've become dowdy. When your best friend's daughter says hello, her eyes glaze over.

When you give the delivery boy a tip, he no longer flashes a smile at you.

And when you catch your reflection in a store window, you hesitate before recognizing the chic woman as *you.*

But don't worry. It won't happen as long as you never stop feeling that you have absolutely nothing to wear.

How to Break the Rules

You'll look like a matron if you insist on putting all the right finishing touches on your outfits. Instead, when the urge to get all dolled up strikes you, wear a costly perfume and get a great new haircut.

- Less chic is more chic. Don't look "expensive."
- For every label you wear, don a nonfashion item. Neutralize the trendy impact of your Gucci, Prada, or Cartier accessories with souvenir scarves, ethnic jewelry, and discount-store undies.
- Unbutton jackets and coats. Sealing off your chest looks too finicky.
- Don't wear your status scarf as a trophy over your coat. Tie it in a hurry. Stuff it. Twist it. Or wrap it negligently.
- Only carry bags you could use as pillows.
- Either do a little less or a little more than what's expected. Either wear no jewelry, or pile on the gold.
- Dare to look lived-in: Remove the temporary stitches that keep your pockets closed.
- Ignore fashion, but never disregard it: Read all about it in magazines— and then do what you want.

the art of
not being right

Y ou'll know that you are no longer self-righteous the day you drop the romantic notion that if only your seventh-grade teacher could see you now, she would be proud of you.

You say good-bye to her. You don't need her approval anymore. From now on, you are on your own.

In the next few weeks following this epiphany, you are likely to make a few upbeat discoveries. You may

What's the difference between being right and not being wrong?

realize, for example, that there is no penalty for not being able to walk on water. That you can make quite an impression by ordering a second serving of strawberry shortcake on a first date. And that being young is great, but being yourself is better.

This is cause to celebrate. But do not look forward to getting on the phone and telling all your friends about it. The demise of one's tendencies toward self-aggrandizement is a quiet, private, and sobering moment of reckoning.

Though you will no longer believe that you must be a paragon of perfection in order to be happy, you still will have to make peace with the fact that some of the best people in your life are fallible, unreasonable—and downright annoying.

Older parents will still fuss too much when they mean to help you. Children will still act like brats when they crave attention. Friends will still talk about themselves when you wish they'd listen to you.

And your mate will still act defensive when you stub your toe or get a headache—as if he or she were to blame.

So, boys still will be boys and hell will still have no fury like a woman scorned—but somehow you will derive no pleasure from the drama of it all.

In numerous cultures priority is not given to the individual, and as a result, presuming that one knows what's best is strongly discouraged.

In India, for example, the principle of nonviolence rests on the acceptance of one's inevitable human fallibility. According to Gandhi, the enemy is within as much as with-

out, and you must seek reconciliation between these two manifestations.

American Indians used to revere a special group of designated "contrary people" whose role was to do the opposite of what everyone else was doing, to remind tribe members that what they considered right and true was a relative notion.

In the Sufi tradition, there is an ancient spiritual discipline called "the Path of the Blame" that exhorts you to go out of your way to justify the questionable actions of others, and even suggests you seek the company of those who don't like you.

The issue here is not forgiveness but practicality. Why should your happiness depend on the exemplary behavior of others? Or on your own upstanding performance, for that matter? You cannot live your life in anticipation of anyone's approval—someone else's or your own.

If you are the kind of person who is

prone to morning-after depressions and post-victory letdowns, take a hint: Acclaim is not the cat's pajamas, after all. Maybe, like the blame-seeking Sufi *Malāmatīs,* you should try to minimize your attainments by concealing them not only from others but also from yourself.

Don't let your ego claim the prize. Deflate your successes with a healthy dose of no-nonsense.

For instance, celebrate a substantial raise by cheerfully taking the garbage out for a week. Compensate for your fifteen minutes of fame by systematically wrapping all your loose coins. Or show you appreciate getting a new client by walking the dog of the old lady next door.

Aware of how the greedy side of the self always gets all the credit for our good fortune, the famous analyst Carl Gustav Jung often greeted friends by asking, "Had any terrible success lately?"

WHEN NOT TO HAVE THE LAST WORD

Between two people in love, nothing is more cruel than the victory of one over the other. At the end of an argument, the winner walks out of the room with a fraudulent look on his or her face. Whether the expression is one of repressed satisfaction or feigned indifference, few grimaces are as ugly. If only for aesthetic reasons, avoid having the last word.

Get into a discussion the way you get into bed with a romantic partner, with the idea that one person should not try to get to the finish line first. Curb your combative nature as much as possible. Ask for help rather than for explanations. Don't look forward to having your way. Research shows that the partner who wins an argument is more likely to send his or her blood pressure soaring up and up.

If it turns out that you were right after all, pour yourself a stiff drink—you'll need it to dull the sting of your sorry triumph.

Among intimate rivals, sex requires just as much finesse in order for it not to turn into a competitive affair. Domesticity would be less fraught with dangers if partners didn't have to measure up to unrealistic standards of romance. What would happen if sex pundits stopped advising us to rekindle our connubial pleasures with scented candles, massage oils, and red satin teddies, and instead extolled the virtues of the chaotic, the disheveled, the hasty intercourse?

No longer glorified in the press, our amorous disports would be nobody's business. Making love would be some marvelous surprise: a passionate struggle to get out of clothes; aimless groping in the dark; yawns, giggles, and kisses; getting violently happy a few minutes apart; and a stray pillow knocking the receiver off the phone just

Love means not ever having to say "I told you so."

before we fell asleep in a slovenly pile.

"Perfection never yet built up an empire," said master strategist Charles de Gaulle. In the same way, getting it right every time never yet inspired Cupid to make a little trouble of his own.

Ten Ways to Say "Bravo"

Telling someone that he is right doesn't make you wrong. It is not a sign of weakness or an admission of incompetence. In fact, spontaneous tributes show how alert you are. Yet most of us are reluctant to acknowledge an astute or insightful remark with a sincere show of appreciation.

To celebrate the pearls of wisdom that fall from other people's lips, try the following comments:

- "You are absolutely right."
- "Can I quote you on this one?"
- "Is that so?"
- "I wish I had said that."
- "Stop. You just said something brilliant."
- "It's so true."
- "You were correct. Once more."
- "I like the way you put it."
- "You've hit the nail on the head."
- "Would you mind repeating what you just said? I'd like to write it down."

A sincere show of appreciation is the shorter distance between two people.

the art of being disorganized

Notice how invariably people slow down when they try to remember something. The slower their movement, the more intense their memory. If they actually stop in the middle of what they are doing, chances are they've stumbled on a startling revelation. If the symptom persists, and they keep interrupting their activities to stare blankly into space, you immediately assume that they are in the

process of unraveling some complicated riddle in the deep recess of their mind.

We all expect Nobel prize winners to be absentminded professors.

Often, slowing down precedes the recovery of a forgotten piece of information. Let's say you are ready to go. You've got your umbrella, the answering machine is on, the cat is fed. Instead of heading for the door, though, you mysteriously put on the brakes. As if in a daze, you check to see if you have your keys, your gloves, your glasses. You remove your scarf and water the plants. You rummage through a pile of newspapers as if looking for a clue. Just as you are about to give up, you remember! It's your mother's birthday. She is probably waiting by the phone for you to call her.

Anytime you either slow down, resist a task, or invent some inane reason for getting behind schedule, pay special attention. Take these organizational lapses as an indication that you are on the verge of some major breakthrough. You are probably entering a zone of creativity. Don't interfere with the process at hand by conjuring up your internal control freak—the homunculus who walks around in your head with a lab coat and a stopwatch.

Be just as patient with yourself when you engage in silly obsessive-compulsive schemes. When you become convinced, for example, that you must reorganize your back issues of *National Geographic* in chronological order. Or when you decide, in an outburst of lunacy, to sort all your old shopping bags by size and color. Or when you attempt to clean your computer keyboard with dipped-in-alcohol cotton swabs.

Heedless bustling is evidence that you are on a holding pattern, waiting for the next available landing strip in your brain.

Don't let appearances fool you. According to productivity experts, taking fre-

Clean your desk so that you can mess it up again.

quent breaks yields higher profits. Progressive companies have noticed that their employees stay more alert and solve problems faster when their work routines necessitate they get up from their desks and walk around.

The frustration generated by repetitive, sedentary tasks causes people to make costly mistakes. But deliberately slowing or interrupting the pace of work requires planning at the corporate level—more than anyone had expected.

A cutting-edge publishing company had to banish coffee machines from office kitchenettes to force people to leave the premises for their caffeine fixes. A high-tech corporation encourages nerds to bring their dogs to work. An architectural firm spared no expense to build an indoor "town," complete with "streets," "parks," and "neighborhoods," to help employees stay on the move.

Ergonomists today recognize that the relationship between comfort and performance is at best elusive. They have all but given up on designing the perfect office chair: The ideal chair is one that encourages getting up as much as sitting down. Rather than supporting your back, buttocks, and thighs, it should prevent you from settling down into semi-immobility. A seat that would periodically eject you would be more efficient—and better for your health overall.

Inefficiency contingency is smart planning. Nomadic by nature, the ancient Persians covered a lot of miles; their empire, the largest of its kind at the time, stretched from Greece to India. Whenever one of their caravans would set out to cross the desert, the first leg of the journey was always short—less than four miles—to give these long-distance travelers time to go back home to fetch the things they had surely forgotten.

Making mistakes is part of getting organized. Think of your blunders as a sign that you are prepping for a long journey.

MAKE A LIST, AND THEN FORGET IT

If being organized is not all it's cracked up to be, why do we insist on it? Because, according to the latest research, feeling in control of one's environment and future strengthens the immune system.

Most likely, when you update your appointment book, balance your checking account, master a new software program, or clean your desk, you reduce the likeliness of getting some dreadful disease.

Improving one's chances of survival is as good a reason as any to write a thorough business plan. The sense of completion and self-fulfillment we experience when a job is well done keeps our medical bills down.

Get a grip, though: There are absolutely no health benefits to being a punctilious bully. Organizational skills should never be used to annoy others.

Compulsive note takers should disguise their entries as casual back-of-the-envelope scribbles.

People who make shopping lists should never consult them at the checkout counter.

Aspiring enologists should take care not to flaunt their "Best Years for Bordeaux" charts at the liquor store.

And folks addicted to palm-top cell gadgets loaded with all the latest interfaces should consider moving to Europe.

Most of our so-called time management gizmos are Rube Goldberg contraptions, clever inventions designed to make everyday life as much trouble as possible.

But, like the insanely complicated yet delightful machines invented by the celebrated American cartoonist, our gallant attempts to marshal disorganization show us for what we are—benign despots rather than dangerous dictators.

Gentle Control over Nature

Rain, wind, critters, dust, weeds, and falling leaves—not to mention floods and tornadoes—conspire to make nature forever untidy.

There is a simple way to bring order to this apparent chaos. The wilderness acquires a human scale when discreet mementos of our presence are left here and there. Indeed, in the right place, the right garden furniture can sometimes do more for a landscape than clippers, pruners, rakes, shovels, and earth movers.

- At the end of a dilapidated pathway, a bench gives the scenery an air of deliberate mystery.
- Hitched to the low branch of a big tree, a swing changes the way you look at the wild meadow beyond.
- On a lawn, a moss-covered stone urn makes weeds, crabgrass, and even molehills look decorative.
- On a patio, a table loaded with flowerpots, bushels of apples, and baskets of vegetables turns an ordinary place into a magical retreat.
- Leaning against an old crumbling wall, a bicycle instantly transforms an overgrown backyard into a picturesque setting.
- On a porch, a rocking chair makes the most rickety house look as pretty as a picture.

Signs of natural and man-made erosion tell eloquent stories.

the art of having taste—not good taste

I f your furniture and possessions look like they came from someone you hardly knew, like a rich great-aunt, your husband's grandfather, or your mother's long-lost millionaire cousin, you probably have what's called taste.

Not good taste, just taste: the grace to take the bounties given to you, and not ask for more.

Whereas good taste is acquired, often the result of

Decoration is the celebration of pleasing disarray.

a long, tedious, costly, and labor-intensive process, straightforward taste comes together out of some sort of carelessness. You don't have to strive for it, keep up with it, or even appreciate it. You can't take credit for it either. It's the most un-American of all distinctions: an unearned privilege—a quality you don't deserve.

To correct this unfair situation that favors laxity, the legal system in this country gives parents the right to disinherit ungrate-

ful children by bequeathing their fortunes to more aggressive and thus deserving retainers or institutions. Unless heirs show the proper filial obedience, the Chippendale breakfront bookcase that has been in the family for generations could end up as part of the permanent furniture collection of the Metropolitan Museum of Art.

In other countries, such as France, descendants are protected by the law. You don't have to be a good son or daughter to inherit the Louis XVI tapestry fauteuil or the *Régence* mahogany desk. Even anarchists end up with priceless antiques in their living rooms. The elegant decor of a French interior has more to do with the civil code than with the sophistication of its occupants.

In America, those among us who aren't to the manner born (and can't tell a sideboard from a buffet) compensate for their bad luck by acquiring good taste. Little do they know that what they believe to be discrimination and worldliness are considered gauche in some circles.

People who have innate taste—but shun good taste—are so secure with their pedigrees that they will serve instant tomato soup in Grandma's antique silver tureen, and light the girandoles before passing around the meatloaf.

Confident that their reputations precede them, they drive their old, beat-up Jaguars ten miles below the speed limit and as near as possible to the middle of the road.

Comfortable with luxuries, they let their dogs, most likely pairs of fierce-looking Rottweilers, chew up the petit point cushions of their eighteenth-century sofas.

Among the privileged few, overt shows of good taste are reprehensible. Everything they do must be effortless. Babe Paley, a socialite and an accomplished hostess, set standards of excellence so high that no one could begin to rival her good taste. A keen observer of social blunders, Truman Capote wrote: "Mrs. P. had only one fault. She was perfect; otherwise, she was perfect."

But do not despair. Today, you don't need inherited wealth to capture the nonchalance of the upper class. Decorating magazines are now showing readers how *not* to flaunt their upward mobility. To emulate patrician elegance, all you need is a couple of props—not the least of them the ubiquitous cashmere blanket casually thrown on the back of a sofa or a chair.

Also heralding the end of obvious good taste are popular decorating vignettes such as art books piled high on chairs and floors, faded bouquets of blue hydrangeas, old bathtubs, mottling gilt frames, sun-bleached shutters, and big dogs.

But the hereditary rich will never be outdone. They are partial to decorative objects most stylists abhor, namely the threadbare Oriental rug, the brick doorstop covered in needlepoint, the crystal table obelisk, and the upholstered chair coming apart at the seams.

HASTE IS THE ENEMY OF TASTE

Even though you may not be silk-stocking material, you can avoid the pitfalls of good taste by living above your means, like a pauper in a palace.

Money was invented to let you splurge on beautiful things. But don't go out and "buy" stuff. Instead "discover" treasures in antiques stores or "find" them in yard sales, flea markets, or auction catalogs. The difference between taste and good taste can be as simple as choosing the right word to describe the pleasure of purchasing something you can't afford.

Another measure of your taste is how much you hesitate before spending the money you have saved. You'll never be accused of being ostentatious if you acquire things slowly. Figure that, on the average, it takes five years to find the right fabric for a sofa. Ten years for perfect champagne glasses. Fifteen years for a great coffee table.

If you do it right, bankruptcy is to be expected some day in the future. You can't do much better than that. There is no greater expression of taste than frugal living in a splendid environment.

A little tousle, rumple, and muss create a sense of place.

A Little Less Bright, Please

Darkness is visually stimulating: Small amounts of illumination look more intriguing and appealing in contrast with shade. American photographer Ansel Adams took some of the most beautiful pictures to date by focusing his lens on the details in the shadows rather than the light.

- During the day, note how a cloud passing in front of the sun can unexpectedly refresh your mood.
- Wait as long as possible in the evening before turning on the lights.
- Display gilded objects in the darkest corner of a room, where they glow rather than shine.
- To increase the scintillating beauty of a crystal chandelier, hang it away from the window, but next to a mirror.
- Note how much more distinctive people look when silhouetted against a soft, dark background. (Anyone can look like they're in a Rembrandt painting when standing in front of rich, dusky velvet curtains.)
- Sit in a dark room and light one candle—just one candle. Its flickering flame will dazzle your soul.

Beware of shiny objects. Seek the comfort of shadows.

the art of not knowing what to do

How come no one ever warned you that life would be fraught with mixed messages? That success, for example, is just another word for a lot more work? That what's called freedom is only the right to do what's allowed? And that you'd derive a lot more pride from your friends' achievements than from your own?

You had to figure it all out by yourself, along with

how to remove white furniture rings caused by wet drinking glasses, where to find a recipe for a cold glazed salmon, and how to apply for a mortgage.

No one told you in advance everything you needed to know to get on with life because you probably weren't ready to listen. Of all the creatures on the planet, we human beings are the slowest to learn. While most animals are born with fully developed brains, the human brain is only 20 percent of its adult size at birth. Before we can absorb information, we must build networks of neurological pathways.

For this reason, childhood plays a critical role in our development. We spend one-fifth of our lives as children, a third becoming mature adults, and the rest of the time bemoaning the fact that we are no longer young.

Whereas a ten-minute-old calf knows all it needs to know to survive for the rest of its life, you and I, after all these years, are still struggling with the most basic abstract notions, such as whether a traveler moving eastward across the date line loses or gains a day, or what is the difference between the liquid and dry measures of a U.S. quart.

The youngest of all species, we have the longest and the most demanding apprenticeship. Because of the diminutive size of our brains and nervous systems in infancy, the learning process is prolonged and tedious. As children, we find going to school to be the object of much anxiety. As adults, we still think of acquiring new knowledge as unpleasant and strenuous.

And yet, we should celebrate our mental incompetence. More than walking upright or being able to talk, befuddlement is our greatest asset, the unique feature distinguishing us from the rest of the primates. Indeed, it is the sum total of our mistakes—which is also called experience—that allows us to learn

Tell me, I'll forget. Show me, I'll remember. Touch me, I'll understand.

from, adapt to, and ultimately survive in the most unexpected and challenging conditions.

In fact, in spite of the difficulties, some folks have become so competent, it's hard to remember they ever were helpless infants. Watch them perform: Within minutes, they can locate on the Internet the best dentist in Siberia, diagnose a rattle in the car as being a problem with the suspension bar, and order a three-course meal, with wine, from a menu written in French.

Very impressive, all right. But nature didn't give us the gift of ineptitude for us to do parlor tricks with it. We were not brought forth naked, without fangs, tails, antennae, claws, fur, scales, or feathers, just to impress our schoolmates with how far we've come.

Weakness is a mighty force in the universe; let's not throw it away. If you want to convince yourself of the power of the meek, think about the hold they have on us.

Within hours of coming home from the

hospital, a newborn baby can disrupt an entire family and send everyone into a frenzy over diapers, bottles, and sleeping schedules.

Folks who don't have a driver's license always find volunteers to take them to the mall, the doctor, or the airport.

Women who dress in tight skirts, wear spiked heels, and carry tiny poodles never run out of men willing to hold the door open for them.

If, for good measure, these weaklings combine ineptitude with charm—a dimple or two, an irresistible smile, a great pair of legs—they have the whole world wrapped around their little fingers.

You are indeed a slow learner if you think that you must overcome your innate incompetence in order to fulfill your destiny as a human being. "I know nothing except the fact of my ignorance," said Socrates, a Greek stonemason who became one of the greatest philosophers of all time.

If you would stop to consider how we are put together—with immature cortexes and almost no inherited reflexes—you would begin to appreciate what unique opportunities were given to Homo sapiens, along with our celebrated opposable thumbs: Not to rule the universe, but to be endlessly curious about it. To take nothing for granted. To ask questions. To go, not knowing where. And to find answers, not knowing why.

WHEN BEING HELPFUL DOESN'T HELP

We all need to be reminded from time to time that we probably don't have what it takes to solve all the problems of the world—but that we are wonderfully equipped to marvel at its existence. To this end, we must get rid of the impression that we are indispensable.

Let go of the concept that people appreciate what you do for them, for instance. True generosity doesn't need gratitude to justify itself. Be helpful to others on your own terms, but let them deal with the outcome.

Don't try to second-guess what's expected of you. Instead, turn the ironies of fate into an excuse to become who you want to be. "Be yourself. It's a tough act to follow," said Katharine Hepburn.

Whenever in a moral quandary, do the right thing. But don't consider that having principles makes you special, superior, or heroic. If, on the other hand, you fail to be as ethical as you think you should have been, don't act surprised. You are only human, remember, neither a saint nor a fraud.

But the fastest way to curb your illusion of mastery is to drop your act in front of others.

Begin by striking the word "entertain" from your vocabulary. When you invite friends into your home, don't think that you have to be the emcee for the evening. On the contrary, act helpless on occasion so that people can come to your rescue and shine in front of you.

Women used to drop their handkerchiefs or their gloves to give amorous suitors a chance to kneel at their feet. Today, running out of ice will do. Send someone to the corner deli in a hurry. Don't deny others the pleasure of waiting on you.

Or come out of the shower when company arrives. Ask guests to pour themselves a drink and keep an eye on the roast while you dry your hair. They'll love the fact that you trust them, and by the time you join them, you'll all be like old friends.

Don't ever assume that you have to be helpful in order to be useful. Your skills are not always required. Why is it so hard for us to accept that sometimes just showing up is enough to brighten everyone's moods?

Let clandestine thoughts frolic in your
fertile imagination.

Why Less Sexy Is More Sexy

The mind is gullible. Whether we experience something or just imagine it, the same part of the brain lights up. A thought alone can trigger a physical response. A glance across a crowded room can set off a chemical reaction. A knowing look is often enough to rev up the libido.

- If tonight's the night, remember that seduction has more to do with what's in your head than with what you wear, or even how you look.
- The less suggestive your gestures but the more graphic your thoughts, the greater your sex appeal.
- Start people thinking by staring at their mouths while they speak.
- Don't deprive him of his thoughts by finishing his sentences.
- Lean forward when she talks to help her concentrate on what she is thinking about.
- While listening, don't fidget, play with your hair, or suck in your tummy: Wait patiently for an enticing repartee to offer itself to you.
- Act casual but feel your insides melt: Your molten imagination is the stuff of love potions.

the art of being silly

illy is the woman who feels a thrill each time she breaks open a fortune cookie.

Silly is the man who is ready to bet that his alma mater will overcome a three-touchdown deficit in the last two minutes of the game.

Silly is the woman who uses expressions like "Perish the thought" or "Ain't we swell."

Silly is the man who refuses to go to the opera

because he always cries at the end of the third act.

Honest and gullible, trusting yet reckless, playful but insecure: That's what it takes to be silly. It is usually the result of a hyphenation of sterling qualities and quirky personality traits.

We are silly indeed when we feel soft and cuddly at the worst possible time. When we try to steal a kiss from someone who is running out the door. When we call back a friend to tell him that we don't have time to call him back.

Take note: Being silly is not the same thing as being self-deprecating or mocking. It has nothing to do with comedy, slapstick, or playing pranks on others. And it is not—I repeat, not—about having a sense of humor. Life is complicated enough. You are not trying to prove anything when you are silly. You just relax, roll your eyes, and that's that.

Unlike stand-up comics, who set out to be funny—and get heckled if they are not—silly people endear themselves to us simply by embracing the role of the "other guy," the archetypal character who bumps into walls and shows up at parties with shoes that don't match.

So next time you are caught talking to yourself in an elevator, you need not apologize. The silent gratitude you generate in your wake when you reveal your most vulnerable side is well worth the temporary blush.

Remember Johnny Carson's show. He was most endearing when one of his jokes bombed and he shrugged his shoulders with a look on his face that said, in effect, "Oh well, I blew it this time, didn't I?"

Flaunting your flaws—not your cleverness—is what will make you popular with your friends.

Today, there is too much emphasis on being witty and ironic. Smart people feel obliged to substitute sarcasm for intelligence.

We are truer to ourselves when we stop making sense.

Artists believe it is their sacred duty to make light of life's most glaring absurdities. And every other magazine headline has to be a pun.

Even having a good chuckle has been medicalized. According to health pundits, twenty seconds of laughter puts your cardio-vascular, muscular, and respiratory systems through a workout equal to twenty minutes of aerobics.

To elicit healthy giggles, exercise instruc-tors are now teaching fitness club members to jump rope, crab crawl, and play leapfrog.

In hospitals coast to coast, clowns push-ing carts loaded with toys—bubble-blowing kits, yo-yos, squirt guns, Slinkys, and whoopee cushions—are doing the rounds along with doctors . . . in the adult wards.

And otherwise straitlaced companies are hiring pricey humor consultants to teach their employees how to make politically correct jokes to ease the tension with the boss.

Enough already. This is just too silly.

Every child comes with a message.

BABY TALK:
WHAT IT MEANS

Being silly comes naturally to all of us. It is the first thing we all do when looking at a newborn baby. One would have to be cold-hearted indeed to stare into a cradle with a stern look on one's face. Women in particular can't resist acting silly the minute they see a cuddly bundle wrapped in a fluffy blanket. They purse their lips and make funny little squeaky sounds. They cackle. They coo. They bleat. They baby-talk.

According to a university study, within as little as forty-two *minutes* after birth, new-borns respond to our pantomiming by imitating our silly facial expressions—smiling, sticking their tongues out, wrinkling their noses, or pursing their lips, as the case may be. It is as if silliness was the most instinctual of all human languages.

Why we make faces at babies is anyone's guess, but it has to be critical, otherwise no one would run the risk of being embarrassed in public by performing such shenanigans. We can only surmise that the encoded information we convey to infants with this goofy behavior is of primary importance to their survival.

Unless, of course, the joke is on us and it is the other way around. Maybe newborns are transmitting information to us through this mysterious behavioral pattern. The grins, whispers, giggles, titters, and suckling sounds we make when trying to communicate with them could be cryptic replies to some mysterious signals coming from the infants themselves. The kids are initiating the dialogue with us—and we are responding to them.

Maybe the peewee creatures are visitors from another realm and their first order of business, as soon as they land among us, is to contact the inner children in all of us.

Spiritual Paradoxes

Why are the greatest comedians some of the saddest people in the world? Why do our eyes fill with tears when we laugh? And why do we say "May I ask a silly question?" when confronting serious issues?

To find the humor in your life, don't shy away from contradictions:

- Explore the richness of your imperfections.

- Understand that you are misunderstood.

- Be good even when you are bad.

- Find the solution by looking for the problem.

- Celebrate your happiness by never questioning it.

- Label the label, before it labels you.

- In order to see, listen. In order to hear, stare at things.

- Cherish the truth, but pardon errors.

"What happens to the hole when the cheese is gone?"—Bertolt Brecht

the art of being neither rich nor famous

Sooner or later, we all will get our fifteen minutes of fame. Friends of your mother will call to say they saw you on TV, though your name was misspelled. The local newspaper will do a cover story on your brother. Your high-school sweetheart will run for office. And the lady next door will be quoted on the travel page.

It means nothing. Once, Gloria Swanson did a

In the end, we become the best person we
could ever be.

ten-minute interview at an airport before
realizing that the journalist thought she
was the famous Hollywood actress Tallulah
Bankhead—who had been dead and buried for
three months.

To quote W. S. Gilbert, from the Gilbert
and Sullivan team, "When everyone is a
somebodee, then no one is anybody."

In order to be perceived as special and
different, rich and famous people today must
strive to shun the limelight and become average folks. They must use their considerable
resources to re-create for themselves all the
trappings of an ordinary existence.

Emulating Marie Antoinette, who played
milkmaid in her make-believe Versailles farm-
house, they go into hiding periodically to
a place where they can pretend to keep
chickens, chop firewood, and make their
own jelly.

But regardless of how much money they
have in the bank, or how much of a buzz they
create when they show up at a club or a char-
ity ball, wealthy folks will never be able to
enjoy the life you and I cherish. Small, reas-
suring pleasures are off-limits to them. You

never see them borrowing books from their local lending library, waiting in line at the post office to buy stamps, or taking the bus down Main Street.

Neither can they entertain the thought of living in a neighborhood where you look out your back window and see laundry swinging on clotheslines, leisurely drying in the sun, or where young men wash their sports cars in their driveways on Saturday mornings to get the attention of the girls next door.

And why be rich if you cannot, on sultry summer nights, drag a card table down to the sidewalk in front of your tenement, unfold a couple of rusty garden chairs, and eat fresh corn with your family by streetlight?

Instead of arguing for the abolition of wealth, social justice advocates should extol the secret satisfactions of not having it all. Perhaps the rich would be tempted to give away their money if they felt that they were missing a lot by being prosperous.

It's about time we share with the more privileged among us how much fun it is to celebrate because the Internal Revenue Service sent a $49.56 refund check.

How liberating it is, when you are flat broke, to lend money to a dear friend who is down and out.

Or how thrilling it is to stumble on your name in print . . . in the phone book.

But one of the saddest things about acquiring fame and fortune is that once you realize that you have plenty, you want plenty more.

Your life is no longer as good as it gets.

You have no use for the expression "enough, already."

And you never tell your friends, "Guess who I saw the other day getting out of her white stretch limo."

Let's not forget that you don't have to be filthy rich to get a taste of glamour. All you need is a fabulous pair of sunglasses and you feel like a million dollars. For good measure, buy a lottery ticket. Now strut to the park to meet the group of senior citizens with whom you play checkers every Sunday afternoon.

To quote the Chinese master Lao-tzu, "He who knows he has enough is rich."

SPENDING IT ALL

In evolutionary terms, it is a lot easier for creatures to cope with shortage than with abundance. Since the threat of a famine has always been greater than the likelihood of a food surplus, we are genetically programmed to gain weight faster than we lose it. People on diets know all too well that when they go off their low-calorie regimens they risk putting on more pounds than they have shed —their bodies overcompensate in anticipation of future dieting attempts.

In the same way, an excess of fame and fortune can be more stressful than a lack of it.

Some rich people understand instinctively that hoarding cash can be a health hazard, and they show great determination in spending their assets. Though their eccentricities are often self-serving, they ultimately choose their servants, their pets, and their guests as the beneficiaries of their munificence.

The Duke of Westminster, Coco Chanel's British lover, had his butler iron his shoelaces every day, while on this side of the Atlantic, a member of the Long Island set had his valet press his newspapers every morning.

On an estate in Oyster Bay, a chauffeur was dispatched to drive his master's exotic ducks to Florida for the winter to save the birds the embarrassment of having to fly south like ordinary waterfowl.

And legend has it that if weekend guests visiting the Rothschilds in their château in France ever fell asleep with their arms hang-

carriage-trade role models. If you ever win a million dollars in a contest, or hit the jackpot in Las Vegas, don't even think of using this windfall to settle your credit card debts. Emulate the rich and famous instead: Spend it liberally on your entourage—or use it to make more debts.

It all comes down to practicing generosity of spirit.

A case in point is Marcel Proust, of *Remembrance of Things Past* fame. A wealthy man-about-town, a prolific writer, and a lavish host, he was also a prodigal tipper, systematically giving waiters an extravagant 200 percent gratuity on top of the bill.

But his largesse went further: He was so eager to share his good fortune with others that he was careful not to invest all his extraordinary talent, charm, and poetic wit into his work. Although his health was fragile, he made a point of always keeping aside time and energy to party all night with his friends.

Give your guests what they never knew they wanted.

ing off the bed, they would wake up with a manicure.

We can all take lessons on how to spend cumbersome sums of money from these

Ten Good Reasons to Be an Ordinary Person

The only difference between a wise man and a fool is that the wise man knows he is a fool. In the same way, the only difference between an extra-ordinary life and an ordinary one is the extraordinary pleasures you find in ordinary things.

1. You can throw away your junk: You are not saving it for posterity.
2. When you fall asleep hugging a pillow, you don't think that you need to talk to your shrink about it.
3. You derive great satisfaction from walking your own dog.
4. You can miss a day at work and the world won't end.
5. You have nothing to hide, and no place to hide it.
6. You don't travel the world in search of what you have at home.
7. You don't have to get all dressed up to go get a sandwich.
8. No one notices whether or not your car is clean, the insides of your closets are neat, and your fence is freshly painted.
9. You don't have to try to make something out of everything.
10. You are enlightened, though you don't know what it means... let alone care about it.

why be happy with more if you can be happy with less?

"Is it possible that progress might be nothing more than the development of an error?"—Jean Cocteau

Perfect moments happen to imperfect people at the most imperfect times.

On a rainy afternoon, while waiting for the local locksmith to show up to retrieve the ignition key you locked inside your car, you have a bowl of homemade chicken soup at the counter of a quaint coffee shop.

When impatiently rummaging through papers in search of the receipt for your defective answering machine, you find an old picture of yourself with your best friend at age ten.

As you put down the receiver after a stressful fight with your sister about family matters, you notice how pretty the garden looks in winter.

Don't hold your breath any longer: Perfect moments happen every day.

Aldrich, Nelson W., Jr. *Old Money.* New York: Vintage Books, 1988.

Ban Breathnach, Sarah. *Something More.* New York: Warner Books, 1998.

De Botton, Alain. *How Proust Can Change Your Life.* New York: Vintage International, 1998.

De Cranz, Galen. *The Chair.* New York: W. W. Norton & Company, 1998.

Forward, William, and Andrew Wolpert, eds. *Chaos, Rhythm and Flow in Nature. The Golden Blade* No. 46. Edinburgh: Floris Books, 1993.

Frank, Thomas, and Matt Weiland, eds. *Commodify Your Dissent.* New York: W. W. Norton & Company, 1997.

Fussell, Paul. *Class.* New York: Ballantine Books, 1983.

Gleick, James. *Chaos: Making a New Science.* New York: Viking Penguin, 1987.

Hawking, Stephen. *A Brief History of Time.* New York: Bantam Books, 1988.

Hoff, Benjamin. *The Tao of Pooh.* New York: Penguin Books, 1982.

Horgan, John. *The End of Science.* New York: Broadway Books, 1997.

Inchausti, Robert. *The Ignorant Perfection of Ordinary People.* Albany, N.Y.: State University of New York Press, 1991.

Johnson, Robert A. *Owning Your Own Shadow.* San Francisco: HarperCollins, 1993.

Kipfer, Barbara Ann. *14,000 Things to Be Happy About.* New York: Workman Publishing, 1990.

Koren, Leonard. *Wabi-Sabi for Artists, Designers, Poets, and Philosophers.* Berkeley, Calif.: Stone Bridge Press, 1994.

Matlin, Margaret. *Sensation and Perception.* Boston: Allyn and Bacon, 1988.

Navel, Georges. *Travaux*. Paris: Stock, 1979.

Osler, Mirabel. *A Gentle Plea for Chaos*.
New York: Arcade Publishing, Inc., 1989.

Schiller, David. *The Little Zen Companion*.
New York: Workman Publishing, 1994.

Stewart, Ian. *Nature's Numbers*. New York:
Basic Books, 1995.

Stine, Jean, and Camden Benares. *It's All in Your
Head*. New York: Prentice Hall General
Reference, 1994.

Sviri, Sara. *The Taste of Hidden Things*. Inverness,
Calif.: The Golden Sufi Center, 1997.

Tanizaki, Jun'ichirō. *In Praise of Shadows*. Stony
Creek, Conn.: Leete's Island Books, 1977.

Tapert, Annette, and Diana Edkins. *The Power of
Style*. New York: Crown Publishers, 1994.

Tenner, Edward. *Why Things Bite Back*.
New York: Vintage Books, 1997.

Thomas, Lewis. *The Fragile Species*. New York:
Touchstone, 1996.

———. *The Lives of a Cell*. New York: Viking,
1984.

———. *The Medusa and the Snail*. New York:
Penguin Books, 1995.

Trétiack, Philippe. *Traité de l'agitation ordinaire*.
Paris: Bernard Grasset, 1998.

VandenBroeck, Goldian, ed. *Less Is More: The Art
of Voluntary Poverty*. Rochester, Vt.: Inner
Traditions, 1991.

Veblen, Thorstein. *The Theory of the Leisure Class*.
New York: Dover Publications, 1994.

Watts, Allan. *Tao, the Watercourse Way*.
New York: Pantheon, 1975.

———. *The Wisdom of Insecurity*. New York:
Vintage Books, 1951.

Winokur, Jon, ed. *Zen to Go*. New York:
Plume, 1990.

In the beginning of my career as a photographer, I was drawn to the idea of perfect imperfection. I tried to capture the special beauty I saw among the women around me. Ironically, this endeavor led me to become a fashion photographer with the task of making the perfect more imperfect. Later, I took the same quest to wild landscapes, gardens in winter, and countries like India. In all of these places, I was hoping that my vision could seek out the beauty even in the least likely of places. It is this experience that I wish to share with you in these pages.

—ERICA LENNARD

Page 2: The ruins of Shah Jahan's tomb, across the Yamuna river from the Taj Mahal, Agra, India. Page 8: Venus of Milo in Charleston Farm House, East Sussex, England. Page 11: Red Fort, Agra, India. Page 12: Ta Prohm Temple, Angkor, Cambodia. Page 15: The Buddha of Compassion, The Bayon, Angkor, Cambodia. Page 16: Isamu Noguchi's studio grounds, Mure, Island of Shikoku, Japan. Page 19: Nude Study V, Paris, France. Page 21: Self-portrait at the Bikaner Palace, Rajastan, India. Page 22: Alexandra at the "Love House," Goa, India. Page 25: Homage to Catherine, in the Paris-Milan. Page 26: Virginia Witbeck and friend on New Year's Eve in Marrakech, Morocco. Page 29: Homage to Simone de Beauvoir, Paris. Page 31: Michele and her daughter, Scarlett, at their restaurant, "Les Deux Cafés," Hollywood, California. Page 32: Mathilda, Kensington High Street, London, England. Page 34: On the set of *Jefferson in Paris*, Château du Champs, France. Page 37: Mathilda in Menerbes, France. Page 39: Installation by Silvy Fleury, Geneva, Switzerland. Page 40: Virginia Witbeck with her new collection, New York City. Page 45: Villa Orsini, Bomarzo, Italy. Page 46: Honen-In Temple, Kyoto, Japan. Page 49: Outa and Michelle, Neuphle-le-Château, France. Page 50: Lise, New York City. Page 53: Homage to Marguerite Duras, Neuphle-le-Château. Page 55: Artist's studio, France. Page 58: Hermann Hesse's garden, Montagnola, Switzerland. Page 61: Palazzo in Palermo, Sicily. Page 62: Inside of Baroque palace near Palermo. Page 65: Brooks Adams with Leo, New York City. Page 66: Chez Marguerite Duras, Neuphle-le-Château. Page 69: Peter and Isabel's wedding, Normandy, France. Page 71: India Scarlett in Santa Monica, California. Page 74: Mak, fashion shoot, New Jersey. Page 77: Emily and Mathilda, Menerbes, France. Page 79: Audrey, New York City. Page 80: Lisa and India, Santa Monica, California. Page 82: Isamu Noguchi's garden, Mure, Island of Shikoku, Japan. Page 85: Canal Saint Martin, Paris, France. Page 86: Portrait of Indian man, chez Jean-François Lesage, Madras, India. Page 89: Vaux-le-Vicomte in winter, France. Page 90: Laurie Frank and Mega, Malibu Beach, California. Page 92: Potager du Roi, Versailles, France. Cover: Sophie in Roberto's apartment, Paris, 1999.